P9-BZO-873

Unusual and Awesome JOBS in SPORTS

Pro Team Mascot, Pit Crew Member, and More

by Jeremy Johnson

CAPSTONE PRESS
a capstone imprint

Edge Books are published by Capstone Press,
1710 Roe Crest Drive, North Mankato, Minnesota 56003
www.capstonepub.com

Library of Congress Cataloging-in-Publication Data
Cataloging-in-publication information is on file with the Library of Congress.
ISBN 978-1-4914-2032-4 (Hardcover)
ISBN 978-1-4914-2203-8 (eBook PDF)

Editorial Credits
Editor: Nate LeBoutillier
Designer: Veronica Scott
Media researcher: Jo Miller
Production specialist: Tori Abraham

Photo Credits
Alamy: Action Plus Sports Images, 17, Diadem Images/Jonathan Larsen, 11, Sindre Ellingsen,
7; Copyright 2013 NBAE (NBAE via Getty Images/David Sherman), 21, (NBAE via Getty
Images/Joe Murphy), cover; Dreamstime: Arne9001, 27, Martin Ellis, 12-13, Sergei Bachlakov,
8-9; Glow Images: Cultura RM/Oliver Furrer, 25; Newscom: Art Foxall, 4, NewsZUMA Press/
Brian Cahn, 29, ZUMA Press/Paul Childs, 19; NHLI via Getty Images/Dave Sandford, 22;
Shutterstock: Action Sports Photography, 15, Christophe Michot, 5, Natykach Nataliia, cover
(background)

Direct Quotation
Page 27, from May 26, 2009, *ESPNChicago.com* article "From MJ to Kobe, an off-court
dynasty" www.espn.com

Printed in the United States of America in Stevens Point, Wisconsin.
092014   008479WZS15

TABLE OF CONTENTS

Play at Work 4

Rodeo Clown/Bullfighter 6

Sports Official 10

Professional Pit Crew Member 14

Ice Technician 16

Golf Caddie 18

Mascot 20

Sports Scout 22

B.A.S.E. Jumper 24

Personal Trainer 26

Sports Commentator 28

Glossary 30

Internet Sites 31

Read More 31

Critical Thinking Using the Common Core 32

Index 32

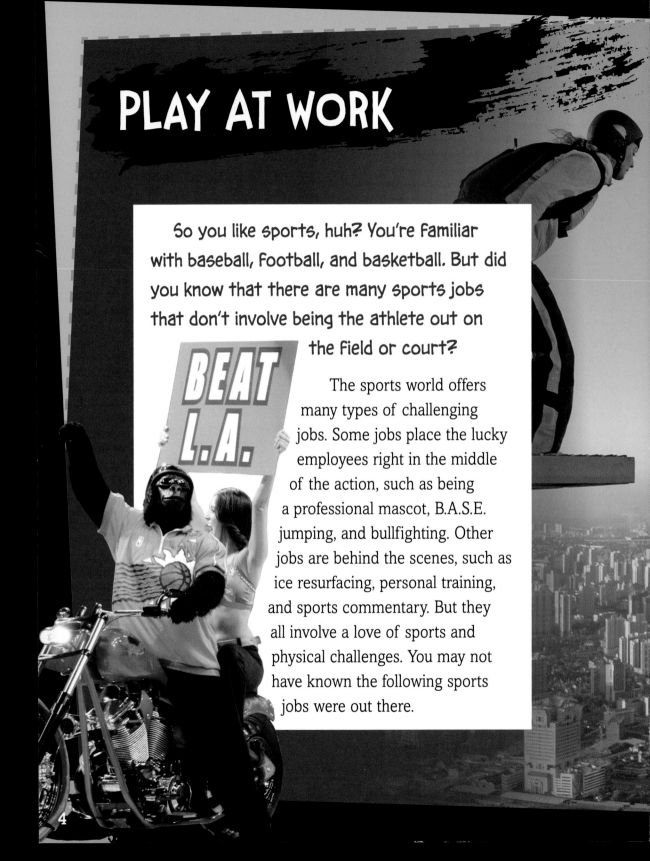

PLAY AT WORK

So you like sports, huh? You're familiar with baseball, football, and basketball. But did you know that there are many sports jobs that don't involve being the athlete out on the field or court?

The sports world offers many types of challenging jobs. Some jobs place the lucky employees right in the middle of the action, such as being a professional mascot, B.A.S.E. jumping, and bullfighting. Other jobs are behind the scenes, such as ice resurfacing, personal training, and sports commentary. But they all involve a love of sports and physical challenges. You may not have known the following sports jobs were out there.

RODEO CLOWN/ BULLFIGHTER

Salary: $150–$500 per event for beginners and up to $1,000 to $2,000 per event for experienced rodeo clowns and bullfighters

Special Skills: acting; good reflexes; bravery

Education: first aid; rodeo knowledge

Prior Experience: a Professional Rodeo Cowboys Association (PRCA) circuit card is helpful

Work Schedule: a typical rodeo season runs from the spring through the fall

HELP WANTED

A bucking and kicking bull has flung a rider off its back. The rider crashes into the dirt. The rules say that a rider needs to stay on the bull for eight seconds before points are scored. The bull rider knows he didn't stay on the bull long enough. But he doesn't care about his score. Right now he sees that the bull has lined him up between his horns. And the bull is ready to charge. The bull rider is in danger. But the rodeo clown and bullfighter are there to help him.

Rodeo clowns entertain crowds by telling jokes and performing **skits**. These activities help make sure everyone is in a good mood and engaged in the rodeo events. The jokes and skits also help calm the audience when there is an accident or emergency.

Bullfighters protect the bull rider. They practice special moves that help guide the animal away from the bull rider. Bullfighters dance in colorful, loose clothing to get the bull's attention. The bull rider can then scamper to safety after falling off the bull.

skit—a short play that is often funny

Rodeo clowns and bullfighters wear face paint, but this is for the crowd's entertainment. An angry bull probably doesn't care about face paint. Rodeo clowns and bullfighters wear protective gear, such as padded vests, padded shorts, and shin guards. They even have barrels they can jump into to avoid being **gored** by an angry bull.

It used to be that the rodeo clown was also the bullfighter. But the two jobs have become distinct from each other. They are now considered separate jobs at most rodeos.

gore—to pierce with horns

YOU'D BETTER BELIEVE IT!

Bulls are colorblind. The idea that they are especially attracted to the color red is a myth. Movement is what gets a bull's attention.

SPORTS OFFICIAL

Salary: : $100,000 per year or more is possible for professional sports officials

Special Skills: good eyesight; quick, dependable judgment

Education: officiating schools and seminars; understanding of the rulebook

Prior Experience: familiarity with the sport

Work Schedule: games are seasonal by sport; individual games last typically one to three hours

A base runner slides into home plate. A receiver catches a football right on the sideline. A basketball swishes through the net at the buzzer. In most sports decisions have to be made quickly. Was the base runner safe or out at home? Were the receiver's feet in or out of bounds? Was the shot made before time ran out? A sports official decides. Those decisions require a careful eye and professional training.

All sports have rules. If a player or coach breaks the rules, the official hands out **penalties**. Officials use whistles, flags, or hand signals when they see someone break a rule.

Some sports, such as boxing and wrestling, need just one official. Other sports need a team of officials, such as football and baseball. Most officials wear uniforms that make them stand out from the players. Depending on the sport, the name for a sports official varies. An official may be called a referee, umpire, or judge.

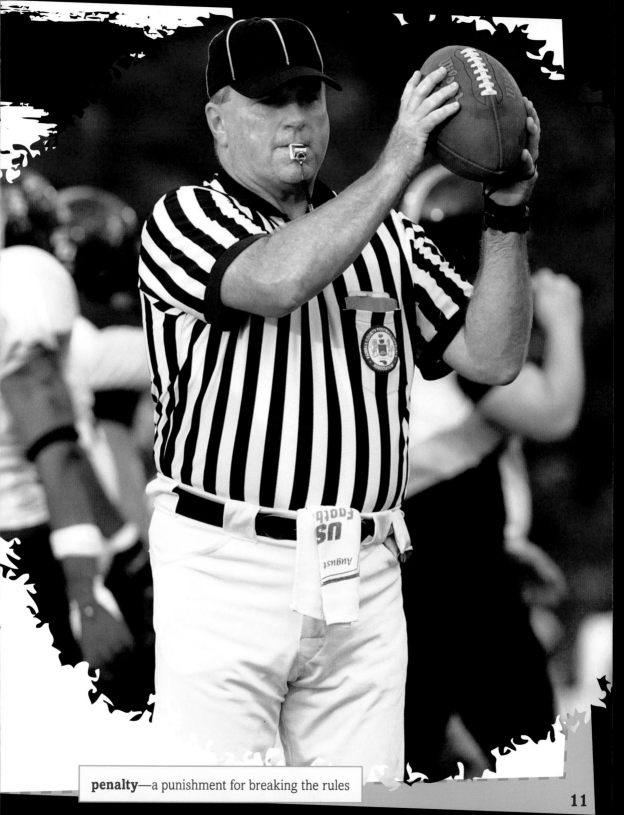

penalty—a punishment for breaking the rules

Sometimes the officials have to keep up with the players to judge the game better. Officials have to be in good physical shape just like the players. Many officials, in their free time, play the sport they officiate. This practice helps them stay in shape. It also helps them learn any new rules to the game as well as remember the old rules.

Officials need confidence in their calls. Confidence is important because some players will scream at the official because they disagree with the call. Sometimes officials have to eject coaches, players, or even fans from the game if they break the rules. Officials need to trust that they are making the correct call. They can't second guess their calls just because someone yells at them.

PROFESSIONAL PIT CREW MEMBER

Salary: $30,000-$500,000 per year plus bonuses for wins

Special Skills: good hand-eye coordination; ability to work quickly and well under pressure

Education: mechanic and trade schools

Prior Experience: various machinist certifications are helpful

Work Schedule: whenever NASCAR events are held

HELP WANTED

It's a **NASCAR** race and the driver in the lead needs gas and a change of tires. The car needs to pull in for a **pit stop**. The driver won't stand a chance of winning the race unless the pit crew does its job fast and well.

During the pit stop, the jackman slips a 20-pound (9.1 kilogram) jack in a notch under the right side of the car. It takes one pump to get the car up high enough for the tires to come off. At almost the same time, the tire changer removes the **lug nuts** with a power tool called an impact wrench. Once the lug nuts are off, the tire changer pulls off the old tires. Then the tire carrier puts the new 25-pound (11.3-kg) tires in place. Then the tire changer tightens the lug nuts on the new tires with the impact wrench.

NASCAR—stands for National Association for Stock Car Auto Racing

pit stop—a break drivers take from the race so the pit crew can add fuel, change tires, and make repairs to a car

lug nut—a fitting on a heavy bolt used on wheels

Once the new tires are on the right side of the car, the jackman lowers the car and the team runs over to the left side of the car and repeats the process. While the tires are being changed, the gas man pours new fuel into the car using two cans of gas which can weigh up to about 80 pounds (36.3 kg) each. Many pit crews are encouraged to develop their strength and speed abilities. Pit crew members sometimes participate in pit crew challenges to fine-tune their skills and fitness. They'll do anything to help their car win.

YOU'D BETTER BELIEVE IT!

In a NASCAR race, a black flag being waved means the driver must come in for a pit stop for consultation. A black flag may come out for many things, such as speeding on pit road, leaking fuel, dragging a bumper, or losing parts of the car on the track.

ICE TECHNICIAN

Pay: varies, depending on if jobs are at community or professional rinks

Special Skills: mechanical and small engine knowledge

Education/Licensure: machinist trade schools are helpful

Prior Experience: knowledge of machinery, ice, and skating is helpful

Work Schedule: whenever skating events are held or ice needs resurfacing

A crack has formed on the ice rink. It's deep enough to catch the blade of a skate, send the skater down hard, and cause an injury. But the ice technician can prevent the crack from deepening. For ice-related sports such as hockey, ice resurfacing machines are needed to keep the surface of the ice smooth. Ice technicians drive the machine. The machine comes out when the ice gets too cut up and pitted for play to safely continue.

The machine has a long razor blade which shaves off the old beat-up surface. It collects those shavings in the tank on top of the machine. Then the machine sprays a blast of warm water on the ice. The blast of water clears out old chips and cracks. The water is then **squeegeed** and vacuumed up. Lastly, another blast of warm water is sprayed on the ice. The warm water freezes well onto the old ice. The result is a clean, level surface. Hockey, figure skating, and other ice sports rely on clean, smooth ice.

squeegee—to spread or wipe liquid material on, across, or off a surface

GOLF CADDIE

Pay: between $1,000 and $1,500 per week
plus 10 percent of a pro golfer's tournament winnings

Special Skills: enough strength to lift a 20- to 30-pound (9.1- to
13.6 kg) golf bag around the course; good eyesight; friendliness

Education: familiarity with golf

Prior Experience: familiarity with rules, math, weather conditions

Work Schedule: 2-5 hours per round

Golf caddies carry golfers' clubs around the course. They suggest which clubs to use and offer other advice. Caddies know golfing terms, such as **fore**, **par**, and **bogey**.

Good caddies are quiet and offer advice at the right times. Caddies need to watch the golfer's swing closely. By paying close attention they can tell the golfers how to improve their swing. Caddies also have to watch the ball after golfers take shots. It is important to know where the ball lands. That way caddies can offer tips for which club to use next.

Caddies must keep the golfer's equipment clean. Caddies always need a new ball ready because sometimes golfers make bad shots. The caddie needs to replace the ball quickly if it is lost.

President Dwight Eisenhower's favorite caddie might have been Art Kennell. Eisenhower would challenge other golfers to see who could hit a ball farthest. Some say Kennell would locate the balls after the shots and kick the president's ball out ahead of his competitor's.

Rory McIlroy (left) takes a tip from his caddy, J.P. Fitzgerald, at the BMW Championship in England in 2014.

fore—a term used by a golfer to warn anyone within range of a hit ball

par—the standard score for a golf hole or course

bogey—a score of one stroke over par on a hole

MASCOT

Pay: $25,000 for beginners to more than $100,000 per year for established professionals

Special Skills: dancing, gymnastics, comedy

Education: attending mascot conventions can be helpful

Prior Experience: public speaking experience is helpful

Work Schedule: 2-3 hours per sporting event

Mascots help audience members bring home happy memories from sporting events. They wear costumes to grab fans' attention. They help the crowd focus their cheers. They also perform skits and dangerous **stunts** during timeouts. If a team plays poorly, its mascot tries to re-spark the fans' interest.

The Minnesota Timberwolves of the National Basketball Association have a mascot named Crunch. He leads the crowd in loud howls. He tosses T-shirts to fans. He goofs off with the referees or opposing players, trying to make them look foolish.

Most mascots also need to have athletic ability. They might **parachute** into stadiums or act out sports scenes in cartoonish ways. Their stunts need to be exciting enough to keep the fans cheering for more.

YOU'D BETTER BELIEVE IT!

The Chicago Cubs briefly experimented with having a live bear, Joa, as their mascot at baseball games. However, the animal wasn't always people friendly.

Crunch soars through the air for a high-flying slam dunk.

stunt—an unusual or difficult feat performed or attempted usually to gain attention or publicity

parachute—to jump from a high place and float slowly to the ground using a large piece of fabric that is strong and lightweight

SPORTS SCOUT

Salary: $60,000 per year or more for established scouts

Special Skills: ability to assess talent

Education: must be familiar with drafting and amateur rules

Prior Experience: a background in the sport they are scouting is essential

Work Schedule: whenever and wherever athletes are playing

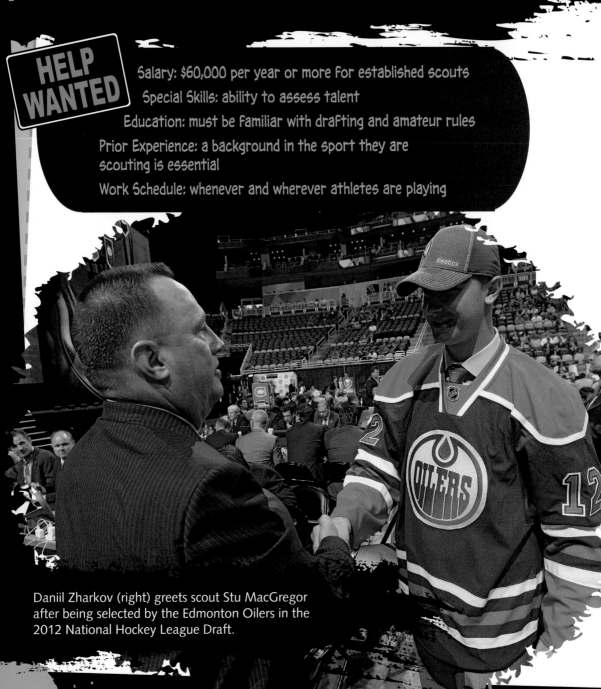

Daniil Zharkov (right) greets scout Stu MacGregor after being selected by the Edmonton Oilers in the 2012 National Hockey League Draft.

The aging quarterback can't throw the ball as far as he once did. He says he will retire after one more season. But the team just signed a wide receiver who can run really fast downfield. So the team plans on finding a quarterback who can throw to the new wide receiver. Who finds the new quarterback? The professional sports scout, that's who.

Most professional sports have scouts. Scouts are people who get paid to watch games. But more specifically they get paid to watch individual players during the games.

Scouts evaluate a player's **statistics** both during individual games and over the course of a season. They evaluate the player's strengths and weaknesses. They take a lot of notes on the player. Then they explain to their bosses why the player would be a good or poor fit for the team.

YOU'D BETTER BELIEVE IT!

In some Latin American countries, scouts watch boys as young as 12 years old play baseball. But a baseball prospect must be 16 years old before signing a minor-league contract.

statistic—a single item of information in a statistical collection

B.A.S.E. JUMPER

Salary: corporate sponsorship pay varies
Special Skills: bravery
Education: safety courses in climbing and parachuting
Prior Experience: sky diving experience
Work Schedule: whenever the opportunity is available

Jumping is quite common in sports. But one sport takes it to an extreme level. B.A.S.E. jumping is the act of jumping off of things high up in the air and then parachuting to the ground.

B.A.S.E stands for Building, Antenna, Span, and Earth. A person either jumps from a building, a tall antenna, a span such as a bridge, or a cliff. Then the person free falls for a short period before parachuting to the ground. After they have jumped from all four categories, they can apply for a B.A.S.E. number. The United States BASE Association issues B.A.S.E. numbers. People are awarded their B.A.S.E. number in the order in which they apply for it. Phil Smith got B.A.S.E. #1 in 1981.

B.A.S.E. jumping is extremely dangerous and has been outlawed in some places. In order to do it safely an athlete must have sky diving experience. More than 240 B.A.S.E. jumpers have died since 1981. Common causes of injury and death in B.A.S.E. jumping include not clearing the platform from which the jumper is jumping and the parachute not opening.

YOU'D BETTER BELIEVE IT!

Whisper, an Australian cattle dog, is believed to be the world's first B.A.S.E. jumping dog. One of Whisper's jumps inspired a 2014 movie called *When Dogs Fly*.

PERSONAL TRAINER

Salary: $30,000 per year or more
Special Skills: physical fitness
Education: various levels of certification
Work Schedule: varies according to client schedules

A high jumper sprints and leaps up over a bar. A baseball pitcher hurls the ball to the catcher. Both of these athletes need to train for their sport. But they need to concentrate on different exercises. The high jumper needs to practice leg exercises. The baseball pitcher needs to focus on arm strength. Both athletes can get help from a personal trainer. Personal trainers help all types of athletes exercise safely and correctly.

Personal trainers help people come up with exercise routines and fitness goals. They know what exercises are best for each person.

Personal trainers know an athlete's strengths and weaknesses. This knowledge helps them plan good exercise routines. Personal trainers often exercise right along with the athletes they are helping.

Michael Jordan, arguably the greatest basketball player of all time, used a personal trainer named Tim Grover. "He said he'd try it out for a month," Grover said of Jordan, "and it ended up being 15 years."

SPORTS COMMENTATOR

Salary: $50,000 per year on average but more well-known sportscasters can make millions

Special Skills: must be very familiar with the sport

Education: journalism and broadcasting schools are helpful

Prior Experience: analysts usually are former players

Work Schedule: 2-4 hours per game

A **sports commentary** team is usually made up of a play-by-play announcer and an analyst. Play-by-play announcers make exciting calls like, "It's Gone! A Home Run!" in baseball, or "He's at the 20 ... the 10 ... touchdown!" in football. They also give the basics of what's happening on the field. They need to speak clearly. It is important that the fans listening at home can easily follow what's going on in the game.

Analysts describe certain aspects of the game. They talk about how and why the players do the things they do. Analysts may describe the way a pitcher holds a knuckleball. They may explain why the quarterback ran with the ball instead of throwing it to a receiver. Usually, analysts are former players who know a lot about the sport. Sometimes the analysts are called color commentators. Their job is to add interest to what could otherwise be a pretty boring game.

YOU'D BETTER BELIEVE IT!

Back in the early days of radio, commentators such as Grantland Rice and Tommy Cowan would read write-ups on the air after the game was over. But they would read them with excitement creating the impression that they were actually reporting live from the games.

sports commentary—the reporting and discussion of sports on radio or television

GLOSSARY

bogey (BOH-gee)—a score of one stroke over par on a hole

fore (FOHR)—a term used by a golfer to warn anyone within range of a hit ball

gore (GOHR)—to pierce with horns

lug nut (LUG NUT)—a fitting on a heavy bolt used on wheels

NASCAR (NAS car)—stands for National Association for Stock Car Auto Racing

par (PAHR)—the standard score for a golf hole or course

parachute (PEHR-ah-shoot)—to jump from a high place and float slowly to the ground using a large piece of fabric that is strong and lightweight

penalty (PEN-uhl-tee)—a punishment for breaking the rules

pit stop (PIT STOP)—a break drivers take from the race so the pit crew can add fuel, change tires, and make repairs to a car

skit (SKIT)—a short play that is often funny

sports commentary (SPOHRTS KOM-uhn-ter-ee)—the reporting and discussion of sports on radio or television

squeegee (SKWEE-jee)—to spread or wipe liquid material on, across, or off a surface

statistic (stuh-TIS-tik)—a single item of information in a statistical collection

stunt (STUHNT)—an unusual or difficult feat performed or attempted usually to gain attention or publicity

READ MORE

Guillain, Charlotte. *Sports*. Jobs If You Like... Chicago: Heinemann, 2012.

Oxlade, Chris. *Sports*. Raintree Perspectives: The Science Behind. Chicago: Raintree, 2012.

INTERNET SITES

FactHound offers a safe, fun way to find Internet sites related to this book. All of the sites on FactHound have been researched by our staff.

Here's all you do:

Visit *www.facthound.com*

Type in this code: 9781491420324

CRITICAL THINKING USING THE COMMON CORE

1. Though rodeos sometimes lead to injuries of the bull riders, fans seem to love them. How do rodeo clowns fit into the danger and entertainment element of rodeos? Do you suppose that the possibility of danger is a reason fans love rodeos? (Key Ideas and Details)

2. Read the text on page 30 and look at the photograph on page 31. How does the athletic ability of mascots and athletes compare? Why might it be important for a mascot to be able to jump high or run fast? (Integration of Knowledge and Ideas)

INDEX

baseball, 10, 13, 20, 23, 26, 28
basketball, 4, 20, 27
boxing, 10
bulls, 6, 7, 8, 9

Cowan, Tommy, 29

Eisenhower, President Dwight, 19

football, 4, 10, 13, 23, 28

golf, 18, 19
Grover, Tim, 27

hockey, 4, 16, 22

Jordan, Michael, 27

Kennell, Art, 19

NASCAR, 14, 15

Rice, Grantland, 29
rodeos, 6

Smith, Phil, 24

wrestling, 10

Zamboni, Frank, 17